note from the editors

The booklet you are about to read was mined from a message Damian Kyle delivered at the 2004 Calvary Chapel Costa Mesa Missions Conference in Murrieta, California. Although the message was specifically taught with the missionaries in mind, the truths herein will encourage anyone who is serving the Lord in any capacity, whether as a housewife raising children or a pastor ministering to multitudes. May you be strengthened in your faith and made joyous in your service.

unappreciated

serving
God
in a
thankless
environment

damian kyle

Let a man so consider us, as servants of Christ and stewards of the mysteries of God. Moreover it is required in stewards that one be found faithful. But with me it is a very small thing that I should be judged by you or by a human court. In fact, I do not even judge myself. For I know of nothing against myself, yet I am not justified by this; but He who judges me is the Lord. Therefore judge nothing before the time, until the Lord comes, who will both bring to light the hidden things of darkness and reveal the counsels of the hearts. Then each one's praise will come from God.

—1 Corinthians 4:1–5

faithful to love

The book of Acts teaches us the history of the early Church. In it we learn about the cities visited by the apostle Paul, and what happened to him as he planted churches in those cities. But in Paul's epistles, the Holy Spirit occasionally gives us glimpses into what was going on inside Paul during those months and years of church planting. We discover what made this great man of God tick, what went on in his heart and mind to keep him faithful in extraordinarily difficult circumstances.

What causes a man to sing praises to God after being savagely, unspeakably, and unjustly beaten, and then cast into the bowels of a filthy, stinking, first century Roman prison? What does it feel like to be pelted with one stone after another until your enemies leave you for dead on the outskirts of a city? What does it feel like to regain consciousness, or to come back from the dead and arise from that rumpled heap, dust yourself off, and not do what I would be tempted to do—run in the polar opposite direction—but instead to walk straight back into that city? I want to know what happens in that kind of heart and mind.

The events described above are not just words on a page. Paul experienced every bit of them. He felt every lash that was laid upon his body, not just one time, but multiple times. He felt every one of those stones hit his body. However, Paul's suffering wasn't limited to physical abuse at the hands of the enemies of the Gospel. What was perhaps his greatest heartbreak came from those under his care in the city of Corinth.

During his second missionary journey, Paul spent eighteen months in the Greek city of Corinth—more time than in any other city except Ephesus, where he spent three years. Corinth was a very, very tough nut to crack, and yet God cracked that city by His Holy Spirit, using the apostle Paul. By the grace of God, he remained faithful there until the church was established.

Imagine having the apostle Paul come to your city for even one day. The tickets would sell out in ten minutes! It would have been astonishing to be a part of the body of Christ that had the privilege of having him minister among them for eighteen full months when his time was so limited, so precious. What an amazing gift.

Directed by the Holy Spirit, Paul gave his life away one day at a time. He labored day and night at tremendous personal sacrifice that the Corinthians might know the Gospel, know of God's love, know of the forgiveness that is found in Jesus Christ, and then understand how to enter into the fullness of the life that is found on the other side of salvation. Although he had birthed the church in Corinth and had served them so sacrificially, the apostle Paul was largely unappreciated there. He was loved by some, but many others there were a constant source of grief.

In Paul's letters to the Corinthians, there is none of the intimacy evident in his epistle to the Philippians. He makes himself vulnerable, but he does so cautiously because he is constantly forced to defend himself and his apostleship. Imagine that—the great apostle Paul having to defend himself to those privileged

Cautious Vunerability ready to defend is apostleship to any challenge

enough to reside under his care. They ought to have been a great source of encouragement and comfort to him, and yet these two letters leave the impression that they never did fully appreciate his gifting or his sacrifice and service to them.

In one of the most pathetic verses in the entire Bible, Paul wrote the following to God's people:

> I will very gladly spend and be spent for your souls; though the more abundantly I love you, the less I am loved.
>
> *—2 Corinthians 12:15*

Today we can hardly believe that Paul would be unappreciated by a body of believers, but it happened in Corinth, and not only there. At the end of his life, Paul stood almost alone in the world. In 2 Timothy 4:16–17, he wrote:

> At my first defense no one stood with me, but all forsook me. May it not be charged against them. But the Lord stood with me and strengthened me.

Paul knew the pain and frustration of pouring his life into a body of believers who didn't appreciate it. Whether or not we can identify with his experience, we need to be prepared for the possibility that God may call us to serve Him in a thankless environment.

faithful to teach

Let a man so consider us, as servants of Christ and stewards of the mysteries of God. Moreover it is required in stewards that one be found faithful. But with me it is a very small thing that I should be judged by you or by a human court. In fact, I do not even judge myself. For I know of nothing against myself, yet I am not justified by this; but He who judges me is the Lord. Therefore judge nothing before the time, until the Lord comes, who will both bring to light the hidden things of darkness and reveal the counsels of the hearts. Then each one's praise will come from God.

—1 Corinthians 4:1–5

According to verse 3 of our text, it would appear that the Corinthian believers spent much of their time judging Paul. Yet, he says, "It is a very small thing that I should be judged by you or by a human court." Here, *judge* means "to examine," or "to scrutinize," indicating that the Corinthians were not looking for good in Paul's life, nor were they seeking to fairly assess his doctrine or conduct. That kind of judgment is more than fair and to be expected. Rather, they were looking for reasons to condemn and criticize. There was a judgmental attitude directed toward Paul. Instead of seeing all the good things he was doing, the Corinthian Christians were constantly putting Paul on trial in their hearts and minds.

I don't know if you've ever heard of people going home from church, and then instead of having roast beef for lunch, they have roast pastor. Sometimes it can be like that. People go home and dissect their pastor, "What did you think of him?" "Oh, I don't know, what did you think?" "Well, did you notice that his tie was crooked, and that point 'B' was weak, and that he stumbled over his words? …" And on it goes.

The Corinthians didn't *want* to like Paul. His two epistles to them give us some glimpses into the reasons why they rejected him. Some people didn't like his simple teaching. They were living in a Greek city, so they wanted the great displays of intellect and human wisdom to which they were accustomed. But Paul refused to feed their appetite for intellectual titillation. In 1 Corinthians, chapter 2, verses 1–5, he says:

> And I, brethren, when I came to you, did not come with excellence of speech or of wisdom declaring to you the testimony of God. For I determined not to know anything among you except Jesus Christ and Him crucified. I was with you in weakness, in fear, and in much trembling. And my speech and my preaching were not with persuasive words of human wisdom, but in demonstration of the Spirit and of power, that your faith should not be in the wisdom of men but in the power of God.

Others didn't like Paul because his style was non-flashy. In their minds, he lacked any great oratorical ability to hold an audience by charisma rather than by the content of what he was saying. They said, "Give us the great orator Apollos. Give us Peter," another very articulate exhorter. "What has God sent us in Paul? A mere teacher—line upon line, precept upon precept." Paul reveals it to be so in 2 Corinthians 10:10, where he tells us what they were saying about him, " 'For his letters,' they say, 'are weighty and powerful, but his bodily presence is weak, and his speech contemptible.' "

What they didn't realize until later (if ever) was that the apostle Paul was a man of enormous intellect and staggering personal charisma. He laid those things aside in Corinth so that the work of God could not be explained away as a product of his natural abilities. He determined to preach in such a way that when God transformed lives, the only explanation would be that the Holy Spirit had done it through His Word. He wanted the foundation of their faith to be the Spirit and the Word.

In addition to those who disliked Paul because of his simple teaching and non-flashy style, others didn't like Paul because he wouldn't allow them to grow comfortable in their carnality. There were a lot of worldly Christians in Corinth, and the apostle Paul could never be comfortable with that situation. It wasn't in him to placate people in their sin. He was the kind of guy who was always pushing people forward in their walk with the Lord in the same way that he pushed himself until the end of his life.

There is a famous old story of a church that had hired a new pastor. He got up the first Sunday and taught an outstanding Bible study. Everybody said, "All right. We picked a winner! Praise the Lord!" As they headed out the back door, they patted him on the back and complimented his message. When he preached the same sermon the following week, the deacons looked at each other and said, "All right, it was good enough to hear twice." So they kept the lid on their concerns. But when the pastor got up and taught the same sermon a third time, the head deacon approached him after the service and said, "Listen, I hope you've got another sermon in your repertoire. You might consider teaching something else." The new pastor answered, "As soon as we obey this one, I'll move on to another one."

There's a little bit of the apostle Paul in that. He never allowed those under his oversight to think that they were spiritual on the basis of what they knew, rather than on the basis of having allowed what they knew to be worked down into the fabric of their lives. In the apostle Paul, the Corinthians got a methodical preacher who wanted their faith based upon the Word of God, and they didn't appreciate it. Despite this fact, Paul loved and taught the Corinthian believers faithfully, and we can benefit tremendously from his experiences in our own service to the Lord.

faithful to serve

There are seven things to notice in our text that helped Paul and that will help us maintain perspective and remain faithful in a thankless environment.

1 First, notice in verse 3 that **Paul considered it "a very small thing" that he should be judged by others**. In the original language, it reads, "the very smallest thing." Paul declared that people's personal opinion of him amounted to nothing. Paul is not being arrogant here. He isn't un-teachable. God had called Paul to Corinth and had told him what and how to preach. If he was forced to choose between hearing the praise of man, as it related to that calling, or the praise of God, Paul states, "The opinion of man means nothing to me. It means less than nothing." Paul had a gift for clarity. I kind of like that.

It isn't that he didn't listen to people. He did. But he did not allow those with a judgmental or critical spirit to get him down. And he did not give undue weight to the unjust criticism of others. That's the qualifying statement. What people with a critical spirit think should be kept a small thing in our hearts and minds. There are times when we are tempted to give undue weight to the assessment of that small group in the church with the critical spirit, but to do that can drive us right out of the place that God has called us to be faithful in serving Him. As long as we know that we're pleasing the One who sent us, we should not be greatly concerned if we displease people.

Notice the second point in verses 3 and 4. It's just as important as the first. Paul says, "**I do not even judge myself**. For I know of nothing against myself, yet I am not justified by this ..." For some of us, by virtue of our personalities, the greatest danger to remaining faithful in the place that God has called us is the opinions and criticisms of others. But for others among us, the critic that lives within and the impossible standard that we establish for ourselves is our greatest danger. The apostle Paul recognized that giving undue weight to his own judgment of himself was as dangerous and destructive as giving undue weight to the judgment of others. We have to recognize that introspection and self-condemnation can diminish our effectiveness, fruitfulness, and longevity as easily as criticism can.

Paul isn't putting down self-examination. He wrote to the church of Corinth, "For if we would judge ourselves, we would not be judged" (1 Corinthians 11:31). Examining ourselves for holiness, purity, and sin is essential. But these verses aren't talking about healthy self-examination. They are talking about our own inability to accurately assess the effectiveness of our ministry or service. Paul said, "I am not qualified to accurately assess my own service to the Lord or to evaluate its effectiveness, even though I know myself, my ministry, and my motivations as well as I do."

The same is true for us. There are rare times when I'm preaching and I feel like I'm running with Eric Liddell in *Chariots of Fire*. It feels effortless. Those are the times when I don't want to leave the pulpit. Everything is so easy, so smooth. The spirit is so right and God is so obviously blessing. Everybody leaves saying, "What a great time we had here today!"

After experiences like that, I wonder how it happened. "How did I prepare?" "What did I say to the Lord just prior?" "What tie did I wear?" I can get as superstitious as a college basketball coach. And then there are other times when I get up there with the same preparation, the same prayer, the same anticipation, and instead of running like the wind, I feel like I'm trudging through three feet of mud. It's called "the romance of preaching." In romance, you never know what's going to happen; in preaching, you never know what's going to happen either. The great tendency, though, is to think the first message is the one that had the greatest eternal impact, and the second one—well, you know, I'll try again another week. But we have no idea what God may have coupled with both of those bits of faithful service by His Holy Spirit, or what He may have done privately in people's hearts. He has all the grace that's needed to make our faithful service fruitful. Spending a lot of time trying to judge our own effectiveness can lift us up into pride or sink us down into condemnation. We need to find that middle ground between the two where longevity in ministry is found.

When a missionary goes to some foreign city, and something happens relatively quickly, almost effortlessly, we judge that as a great success. And then someone else goes to another place, trudges, works, and labors anonymously with so little appearing to happen. Someone might ask, "Who got saved in your thirty years of ministry in that remote city? Ha! Only one person." But, he just happened to be the next Billy Graham of Central and South America. *We don't know what God is doing.* But we judge it. We come to conclusions about ourselves and our own faithfulness, about what is and what is not successful, when it's the same faithfulness. God knows it's the same faithfulness, and He's just as pleased with both works. *God is pleased w/our heartfelt faithfulness*

So we have to be careful as the apostle Paul was careful. He gave as little weight to his own natural opinions and self-criticism as he gave to the natural and fleshly opinions of others. He recognized that he was every bit as capable of misjudging himself as anyone else was. We have to be careful not to condemn ourselves right out of the ministry.

(3) Third, notice in verse 4 that he said, "**But He who judges me is the Lord**." Paul entrusted all judgment to the Lord because only the Lord knows the whole story. Have you ever judged someone or something without knowing all the facts? How well did you do? It's tempting to think we have the *gift* of looking at a situation and understanding all that is necessary to judge it. Jesus commanded us not to judge. If we defy Him and decide to judge people or situations outwardly, ninety-eight percent of the time, we discover that we're wrong. We have no ability to do it. But God sees everything. He has all the facts. He knows what nobody else knows, even concerning us. He knows all the heart issues. He knows all of our motives, and one day all of that will be brought out.

In verse 5, Paul alludes to the fact that all of the dark motives for criticizing him—the envy, jealousy, and carnality—will one day be revealed. With these kinds of motives, no believer ever comes along and says, "Listen, I am a carnal Christian, and out of my carnality, I'm going to resist the apostle Paul." No one in such a condition is that transparent. Their opposition is always carefully couched in spiritual terms and noble speech. "It's only because I care about the church that I'm trying to replace Paul with Apollos or Peter."

But every motive of the heart—both *his* heart and his opponents' hearts—will be exposed at the Bema Seat of Christ (the reward seat). In that day, there will be a lot of surprises, according to the apostle Paul. There will be praise for people we thought had no praise awaiting them, and some of the people we thought had tremendous praise awaiting them will turn out to have been the biggest pains in the neck. Many in the body of Christ in Corinth will find that there's nothing for them. They'll have gotten into the kingdom of God, but they'll be tinged with the smell of smoke,, having barely gotten in for all of eternity. What a shame.

Very early in my Christian life, I heard Greg Laurie say, "If you take care of your character, God will take care of your reputation." It's true; He is faithful to do it. Maybe not in a week, or even in six weeks, but He will always do it. However, if the devil identifies you as someone who tries to put out every single fire started by people that don't necessarily like you, he will light so many fires that your gravestone will say, "The man who spent his life putting out fires and never got to his ministry." Paul had the ability to say, "I entrust other people's opinion and my own to the Lord; I entrust all judgment to Him." When we know that our integrity is right, that God is purifying our motives and sanctifying us more and more every day as we serve Him, then we can trust all judgment to Him.

Fourth, notice in verse 1: Paul reminded himself that he was a servant of the Lord Jesus and that he needed to remain a servant, wherever the Lord decided to put him. He says, "**Let a man so**

consider us, as servants of Christ. …" The word Paul uses for *servant* here is unique for him. When he speaks of himself as a servant, he usually uses the word *doulos*, meaning, "bond-slave." But here he uses the word *hyperetes*, which means, "under-rower." It appears elsewhere in the New Testament, but this is the only time Paul uses it.

Perhaps you remember Charlton Heston looking fit and tan rowing on one of those great Roman battleships in the movie *Ben-Hur*. Seeing that, you might think, "Wow, being a slave with an oar looks like a pretty good workout program—plenty of sun, lots of ventilation—he's looking pretty good in that movie." In reality, those ships had two decks of slaves with oars and chains, and it was no fun being a slave on any deck, not even on the upper deck. If it was no picnic on the upper deck, it was really miserable on the lower deck. Not only were men chained to their oars and made to row beyond exhaustion, but they did it with no ventilation and no sun, just the stinking smell of flesh all around them. To be an under-rower meant dismal circumstances.

In Paul's day, to take the position of under-rower was to take the lowest position of all. In a sense he says concerning Corinth—and the Holy Spirit has recorded it so that we know it today as well—"I'm not only chained to the ship, I not only have the blisters, the aching back, and the exhaustion common to all service for the Lord, but in Corinth the environment has its own challenges. There is no spiritual or emotional daylight and no fresh air."

Jesus gave us a tremendous example of servanthood the night before He went to the cross. He took a basin and a towel and He washed the disciples' feet in the upper room. Sometimes

I fall far short of His example, and I realize that I'm reacting like a *prima donna*: "Wait a second. They can't tell me what to do. I'm the senior pastor here! They're treating me like a servant instead of a preaching machine." But of course, the famous saying concerning servanthood is, "You know how well you are doing in your seminary class on servanthood based upon how you react when people treat you like a servant." Paul understood that he was a servant. You and I need to remember that as well.

Missionaries and pastors aren't the only ones who serve ungrateful people. There can be a lack of appreciation as we serve the Lord in our marriages. What spouse hasn't felt unappreciated at one time or another, even in the best of marriages? Some people are in completely one-sided marriages. One person does all the giving and the other person does all the taking. You do all of the giving. He does all of the taking. You do all of the giving. She does all of the taking. If that describes your marriage, you understand Paul's declaration to the Corinthians—"The more abundantly I love you, the less I am loved."

It happens to parents, too. As you raise that difficult child, or that good child during that difficult period, there is no appreciation expressed, only the endless struggle for the control of your household. If you are experiencing that, you understand Paul completely.

Or as a young person, you love the Lord. But you are living in difficult circumstances—at school, or maybe in a household where no one else is walking with the Lord. One would think that in this day and age, when godly young men and women are difficult to find, your faithfulness would be deeply appreciated. But because evil is called good and good is called evil in today's world, even those who ought to be admired live with no positive reinforcement at all.

Or as an employee, the attitude of your boss might be, "What have you done for me lately?" Yet, the Lord has placed you in that job for His glory, even if there is never an ounce of appreciation expressed toward you.

I think of other areas of service to the Lord. Perhaps you serve in children's ministry, where there can be an absence of appreciation. It can be tempting to think, "I'm done with this. It's not the kids. It's just that nobody ever seems to appreciate what I do. I don't need the aggravation."

Or maybe as a worship leader, or someone who is part of the clean-up ministry, or as a missionary, you understand what it is to be unappreciated. Or maybe in obedience to the Lord, you are running for public office, the school board perhaps, and no one seems to appreciate it. The great tendency is to think, "Who needs this stress and ingratitude? I'm out of here."

Like Paul, you are doing what you know the Lord has called you to do, and yet it's a challenge. The apostle Paul believed that, as a servant, he wasn't too good for any circumstance that God chose to put him in. If he wasn't too good, then neither am I, and neither are you.

Remembering that we are servants also protects us from self-pity—an enemy that can endanger the longevity of our ministry. Because self-pity is a great hazard, the apostle Paul reminded himself that he was a servant. While in Philippi or Thessalonica,

Paul may have thought, "Here I feel like a bond-slave." But in Corinth he said, "I feel like an under-rower." It can be very tempting to look around, especially after we've been serving for a while, and begin to think, "I don't need to put up with this." But Jesus, who bought and paid for us, is free to spend our lives any way He chooses.

Here's the upside: we can be confident that our lives are not being wasted where God has placed us. God will not even waste the remains of a miracle. Remember the multiplication of the five loaves and two fish? Jesus had the disciples gather up the leftovers and put them into twelve baskets. If I were Him, I would have said, "It was a miracle! Throw it away. We'll do it again tomorrow." But God doesn't even waste miracles. All the leftovers were gathered up. And if He won't waste what is temporal, He won't waste a day of our lives, much less a week, a month, a year, or all the days of our lives. He knows the best ways for the lives of His children to be spent.

Fifth, notice in verse 1 that Paul says, "Let a man so consider us, as ... stewards of the mysteries of God. **Moreover it is required in stewards that one be found faithful**." Paul committed himself to being a faithful steward where God had placed him. A steward is a little bit different from a servant. If you accumulated a certain amount of wealth in that ancient culture, then you would buy slaves to act as stewards overseeing your wealth or property. But they didn't act independently of their master, saying, "My master has given me his portfolio worth sixty million dollars. I'll go ahead and invest it as I see fit." The master would come and say, "This is what I want you to do with what is mine, and when I come back, I expect it to be done." Nobody wanted a steward that was a maverick—"I bet it all on tech stocks." "You did what?!"

Paul was given all the truths of the New Covenant to deliver to the whole world. Essentially, God said, "I'm giving you the most valuable thing in the world, and when I come back, I want you to be found faithful in having done My will in regard to it." According to Paul, a steward doesn't have to be the most talented, the most eloquent, the most amazing person, or anything like that. The one thing that is vital in a steward is faithfulness to the Master. Paul persevered in the difficult atmosphere of Corinth because God had called him there for eternal purposes.

Sooner or later, it all comes down to faithfulness. I don't know about you. You probably entered the ministry in service to the Lord far less carnal than I did. I was very carnal, and still have a long way to go, but I'm further along than when I began. I am so grateful that when the Lord called me to start a church in Modesto, California, it was several hundred miles away from Southern California and Pastor Chuck Smith. That way he didn't know about all the stupid things I was doing!

We begin with a lot of motives that can be selfish—with a lot of "me" in them. A lot of them can be people directed (those are a little nobler than the "me" motives). But sooner or later, it always comes to faithfulness. God always brings us to a place in our service to Him where we say, "I would not do this for myself, I would not do this for another human being, but I will do it for You." We respond in love, which becomes the single great motive for our service and will carry us through the Corinthian kinds of experiences that are part of all of our lives. Whether or not our ministry looks like what we did or did not expect it to look like, we know that we need to be faithful in it because we would be disobedient to the Lord if we quit.

I have a recurring dream that seems to surface when there is a lot going on—maybe spiritual warfare, or some ministry pressure or problem—or when everything comes together all at once. In my dream, I'm not a pastor anymore. Instead, do you know what I'm doing? I'm retrieving shopping carts in the Target parking lot. I don't mean to offend anyone who works at Target. I'm not talking about being a cashier or a manager. I don't want that much pressure. My dream is to put on my parka and for eight hours a day, go out there, smile at people, and collect carts. I've got my little place, and not a problem in the world. Nobody knows I exist, and nobody cares. I'd eek out my little existence and then go to heaven. I know I'd be miserable in forty-eight hours, but let me dream!

Faithfulness to Him keeps us in the place of service. Paul realized that as difficult as Corinth was for him, God had called him to serve there, and as miserable as the circumstances were in many respects, he would continue to serve. Maybe you need to freshly commit to being faithful in the place where God has called you to be—in that one-sided marriage; with that ungrateful child; in that thankless job or ministry; wherever it might be—do it as an expression of worship to the Lord. *Faithfulness, not quitting is my worship*

If you're in that place where you've had all these other motives, everything is hard, things are being burnt off of your life, and you realize, "I wouldn't do this for people, or for myself anymore. If those were the motives, I'd quit," I want you to know you're right on schedule. We all come to that place. That's when you say, "I'll do it to be faithful to You, Lord," and then commit to continue serving with that motive. ✓ ⊢ That's me 20/9/14

There's a saying that I use, and it's not great. I'm not going to get famous or rich off it, but it goes something like this, "If *I* can't quit, *you* can't quit." Kind of catchy, isn't it? It's biblical, but that's another study. One of the leaders in our church is stepping out into a new area of ministry within the fellowship, and it represents quite a step of faith for him, so he said to me, "I'm so afraid." Join the crowd! I responded, "I'll tell you what, if God accepts that excuse, let me know. He wasn't the last time I checked; and if He's accepting it now, I want to at least know it's an option." But He doesn't. He calls us to faithfulness.

Sixth, notice in verse 5 that Paul stayed conscious of the Lord's return. He says, "**Therefore judge nothing before the time, until the Lord comes**, who will both bring to light the hidden things of darkness and reveal the counsels of the hearts."

The apostle Paul was doubtless the greatest missionary in the history of the Church next to the Lord Jesus Himself. When you read the epistles that he wrote inspired by the Holy Spirit, you find that there's an almost constant reference to eternity—to life beyond this life—which tells me that his eternal perspective was one of the keys to his effectiveness and longevity as a missionary. He realized that all of *this* life that we're living, all of this service that we give to the Lord, ends one day in a very real heaven—a heaven that is more real than the building that surrounds you and the seat you are sitting on. One day we will stand on the glassy sea and cast our crowns before His throne. Paul never lost sight of that future. He said, "For I consider that the sufferings of this present time are not worthy to be compared with the glory which shall be revealed in us" (Romans 8:18).

In 2 Timothy 4:5–8, he elaborated:

But you be watchful in all things, endure afflictions, do the work of an evangelist, fulfill your ministry. For I am already being poured out as a drink offering, and the time of my departure is at hand. I have fought the good fight, I have finished the race, I have kept the faith. Finally, there is laid up for me the crown of righteousness, which the Lord, the righteous Judge, will give to me on that Day, and not to me only but also to all who have loved His appearing.

The word *finally* jumps out at me from verse 8 because in that word the apostle Paul reveals part of what drove him and what kept him through all those difficult years—the day that he would stand in heaven.

Years ago, I heard Warren Wiersbe say that for the Christian "heaven isn't just a destination; it is a motivation."[1] That was true of Paul, and it needs to be true of us.

C. S. Lewis similarly wrote, "If you read history you will find that the Christians who did most for the present world were just those who thought most of the next. ... It is since Christians have largely ceased to think of the other world that they have become so ineffective in this."[2] The eternal perspective—it all ends there. This life is the preparation. It's the race, not the finish line.

But eternity is something that is kind of hard to get your mind around. A man named Hendrik Willem van Loon wrote something that I enjoyed reading concerning eternity:

High up in the North in the land called Svithjod, there stands a rock. It is a hundred miles high and a hundred miles wide. Once every thousand years a little bird comes to this rock to sharpen its beak. When the rock has thus been worn away, then a single day of eternity will have gone by.[3]

All right! Eternity is a long, long time—it's worth living for, and it's worth serving for.

Finally, in verse 5, Paul says, "**Then each one's praise will come from God**." What kept him from bitterness and self-pity? What kept him full and usable in that setting? Paul was confident that at the end of such a life was the greatest reward that anyone could ever have, and that is to receive praise from God.

I have an appointment to stand before the Lord Jesus one day and so do you. I desire to stand before the crucified One, to look into His eyes, and to hear from His very lips,

> Well done, good and faithful servant, you were faithful over a few things, I will make you ruler over many things. Enter into the joy of your lord.
>
> —*Matthew 25:21*

A life that does not hear those words cannot be considered successful. It is only the life that hears those words that will have been well spent on planet earth. And yet, for Paul to one day hear those words from the Lord meant that a long period of his life would be spent in the most difficult circumstances—perhaps every bit as difficult on the inside, within the heart and mind, as stoning was on the outside.

be found faithful

Perhaps like the apostle Paul, God has entrusted such an experience to you, and your circumstance is completely one-sided. You do all of the giving every day, and someone else does all of the taking. And your giving is met with ingratitude. Remember the seven things that helped the apostle Paul maintain perspective and remain faithful. First, don't let the unjust criticism of others drive you out of your service to the Lord. Second, don't judge yourself; you know as little as they do. Third, entrust all judgment to the Lord. Fourth, remain a servant, an under-rower. None of us is too good for the place that God has called us to spend our lives. Fifth, be careful of self-pity, and stay faithful in whatever situation you find yourself in. Sixth, there is praise coming your way that will make you forget all about its long absence in this life. And seventh, remember that the Praise Giver may come today. So, be found faithful.

> Therefore, my beloved brethren, be steadfast, immovable, always abounding in the work of the Lord, knowing that your labor is not in vain in the Lord.
>
> *—1 Corinthians 15:58*

notes

[1] Wiersbe, Warren. *A Child of God: Your Guide for the Adventure* (Nashville, TN: Thomas Nelson, 1996), Ch. 18.

[2] Lewis, C. S. *Mere Christianity* (New York, NY: HarperCollins Publishers, Inc., 2001), 134.

[3] van Loon, Hendrik Willem. *The Story of Mankind*, online edition. Retrieved April 30, 2004, from www.worldwideschool.org/library/books/youth/history/TheStoryofMankind/chap2.html.

other materials available

Visit Calvary Chapel Modesto's web site for audio messages by Pastor Damian Kyle:

www.calvarychapelmodesto.com

Audiotapes are also available by calling 209-545-5530, by writing to 4300 American Avenue, Modesto, California 95356, or by e-mailing:

tapelibrary@calvarychapelmodesto.com

The audiotape this book was taken from can be purchased by calling 800.272.WORD, or by writing to Chapel Tapes, P.O. Box 8000, Costa Mesa, CA 92628. The tape number is: MCO0045E: Missions Conf. '04.